Reflections on the Synoptic Gospels

Sharon E. Jones Roberts

Copyright © 2025 Sharon E. Jones Roberts

ISBN: 979-8-218-62014-1

All rights reserved. No part of this publication may be reproduced, stored in a retrieval system, or transmitted in any form or by any means, electronic, mechanical, recording or otherwise, without the prior written permission of the author.

Majestic International Books, Chesapeake, VA

Majestic International Books. Com
2025

Lovingly dedicated to Prophet William Saunders Crowdy

Table of Contents

Preface vii
Introduction 1
The Seven Keys with their Subsequent Interpretations 5
Creation of the New Testament 7
Historical Context of Second Temple Judaism 13
Historical Context of the Greco-Roman World 23
The Gospel of Mark 31
The Gospel of Matthew 41
The Gospel of Luke 51
Textual Criticism and Criteria for Historical Reliability 63
Conclusion 69
Bibliography 71
Notes 73

Preface

The information in this publication was used to facilitate a course on the Synoptic Gospels for ministerial recruits and recently ordained ministers. For that privilege and this, I give thanks, praise, and all glory to God. The purpose of the course was to introduce the participants to the Synoptic Gospels as first century literary and historical writings. The course lectures largely were derived from Bart Ehrman's New Testament textbooks: *The New Testament: A Historical Introduction to the Early Christian Writings* and *A Brief Introduction to the New Testament.* The course was offered by the William H. Plummer Seminary of Church of God and Saints of Christ, Temple Beth El, Suffolk, Va, International Headquarters. Nevertheless, the material and views presented in these pages do not represent the official doctrine or theology of the seminary or the religious organization.

Introduction

Even though the Christian religion did not exist when the texts of the New Testament were written, New Testament scholars identify the authors of the New Testament writings as early Christians. At the same time, they generally acknowledge that the New Testament authors and the communities for whom they composed their writings were actually first century Jews. Scholars often state this nonchalantly without emphases or elaboration. One scholar who does expound on this point is Julie Galambush in her book, *The Reluctant Parting: How the New Testament Jewish Writers Created A Christian Book.*[1] That the Synoptic Gospels and other books of the New Testament originated within the historical context of Second Temple Judaism is far from trivial. Indeed, the fact that the New Testament texts *were* written by first century adherents of Second Temple Judaism for their respective first century Jewish communities is the central premise of this work.

The Jewish origin of the New Testament is particularly significant to Church of God and Saints of Christ, Temple Beth El which observes the ancient Israelite tradition of prophetic Judaism. The seven founding principles that Prophet William Saunders Crowdy received in the vision that eventually led to the establishment of the congregation includes scriptures from the Old and New testaments. These seven principles, that we call the Seven Keys, were Divinely revealed to Prophet Crowdy in the literal shape of seven keys. Each key contained a statement and biblical reference. The keys Divinely connected the Judaic tradition of ancient Israel in the Hebrew Bible (Old Testament) to the Second Temple Judaism in the New Testament. Moreover, the keys are the key to the distinct prophetic Judaism of Church of God and Saints of Christ, Temple Beth El.

The recognition of the New Testament writings as first century Jewish writings also confirms that Prophet Crowdy reestablished a Judaic and not Christian way of life. As reported in *The Truth He Brought: William S. Crowdy a Prophet of God,* during the twelve years that Prophet Crowdy served as the congregation's initial executive leader he did not require the observance of Christian holidays such as Christmas and Easter.[2] Instead, in 1899, the congregation began observing the festival of Passover and Feast of Unleavened Bread as described in Exodus 12.[3] In 1901, the observance of the Israelite New Year based on Exodus 12:2, and in 1904 the Fast of Tebeth found in Zechariah 8:19. During this formative period, Prophet Crowdy also taught the congregation to use the Hebrew names for the months of the year. Hence, it is more than fitting for his corporate and theological descendants to seek to understand the New Testament writings in their original historical context of Second Temple first century Judaism before the texts were appropriated and interpreted by Christian theologians of later centuries.

We began this endeavor with a brief explanation of how the New Testament came to exist. We then discussed the historical contexts of

Second Temple Judaism and the Greco- Roman world, before examining the main themes and features of each Synoptic Gospel.

The Seven Keys with their Subsequent Interpretations

1st Key - Church of God and Saints of Christ - I Corinthians 1:2
Interpretation: Divine ownership

2nd Key – Wine is forbidden to be drunk in the Church of God and Saints of Christ forever – Leviticus 10:9
Interpretation: Sobriety and Charity

3rd Key – Unleavened bread and water for Christ's body and blood – Matthew 26:26-28
Interpretation: Purity

4th Key – Foot washing is a commandment – John 13:1-8
Interpretation: Humility

5th Key – The Disciples' Prayer – Mathew 6:9-14
Interpretation: Supplication

6th Key – You must be breathed upon and saluted into the Church of God and Saints of Christ with a holy kiss – John 20:22; Romans 16:16
Interpretation: Love

7th Key – The Ten Commandments – Exodus 20:1-18
Interpretation: Unconditional Surrender to God

Creation of the New Testament

The New Testament is the canon of Christianity. **Canon** is a collection of text recognized as authoritative. The word stems from a Greek term for a ruler or straight edge, and became a metaphor in Greek culture for accuracy, definiteness and truth. Canon is not identical to scripture. Scripture has been defined as a semi-durable, semi fluid, slowly evolving conglomeration of sacred texts (not necessarily in written form) used by members of a religious tradition over hundreds, even thousands of years. Canon, on the other hand, is the result of the intentional designation of specific texts as definitive. While there are references to the sacred writings of other religions as canons, only Judaism, Christianity and Islam have created collections of writings that their respective adherents recognize as authoritative. All religions may have sacred texts, but not all sacred texts constitute a canon like the New Testament.[4]

The creation of the New Testament as the Christian canon occurred over a protracted period beginning in the second century and extending into the fourth century and beyond. The twenty-seven texts were strategically selected from hundreds of other writings about Jesus that were produced by groups with diverse views about him and his teachings. The New Testament was created by the group known as the **Proto-Orthodox**. Proto the Greek word for first and orthodox meaning right opinion. The first record of the twenty-seven writings as a proposed canon was in a 367 CE letter by **Athanasius,** the Proto-

Orthodox Bishop of Alexandria.[5] By the end of the fifth century, Athanasius' list had been universally adopted as the Christian canon.[6]

Historians classify second century early Christians, or the Jesus Movement as Julie Galambush refers to them, as either Proto-Orthodox, Jewish Christians or Gnostic. Proto-orthodox believed that Jesus was human and divine, one being and not two, whose disciples recorded his teachings in books which they transmitted to their followers.[7] Jewish Christians like the **Adoptionists** and **Ebionites** believed that Jesus was fully human, adopted as God's son at his baptism, and then empowered by God to do miracles and to teach God's truth. His crucifixion fulfilled his divine commission as a willing sacrifice for the sins of the world, a sacrifice that ended the need for any further sacrifices. After his death, they believed that God raised him from the dead and he ascended to heaven to reside with God. These groups observed the Jewish law, and required non- Jews who wanted to be true followers of Jesus to convert to Judaism. For men, this meant being circumcised, and for men and women, it meant keeping the Sabbath, and kosher food laws. They based their beliefs on a text similar to the Gospel of Matthew minus the first two chapters. They did not recognize Paul as an apostle, but considered him a **heretic**: a term applied to someone who believed differently from what was considered the correct or orthodox view.[8]

Unlike the Jewish Christian groups, **Marcion** was a second century **Docetist** who maintained that Jesus was fully divine and only appeared to be human. While Docetists were **Gnostics,** Marcion's theology was so extreme that his group usually is described separately from other Gnostics.[9] The Marcionites believed that the God of the Hebrew scriptures and the God of Jesus were different Gods. The God of the Hebrew scriptures, they claimed, was a God of wrath. The God of Jesus was a God of mercy and forgiveness who sent Jesus to save people from the wrathful God of the Hebrew Bible. The group was located throughout the Mediterranean region, but primarily in Asia Minor (modern Turkey). They considered Paul Jesus' only true apostle and accepted most of his writings as authoritative. Marcion was one of the first to provide a canon for his followers. His canon included some version of the Gospel of Luke and ten epistles thought to have been written by Paul. His canon did not include Hebrews or the Pastoral Epistles of I&II Timothy and Titus.[10]

The third early group, the **Gnostics**, were located in major urban centers in Egypt, Syria, Asia Minor, Rome, and Gaul. They are defined as ancient religions, some closely related to Christianity, which maintained that elements of the divine were trapped in the evil world of matter and could only be released by acquiring the secret gnosis, generally thought to be brought by an emissary of the divine realm. Some Gnostics agreed with the Marcionites that Jesus was fully divine and associated with a different God than the one who created the material world. Others believed that Jesus was both human and divine. Like the Adoptionists, they thought Jesus was a righteous man whom

Christ entered at his baptism empowering him to heal and teach. Christ then departed from him just before his crucifixion. For them, Jesus was the divine emissary who came into the world to impart the secret knowledge (gnosis) people needed to escape the world, which they considered evil along with the God who created it.[11]

Prior to 1945, information about the Gnostics primarily came from the writings of the Proto- Orthodox **Apostolic Fathers,** and other Christian **Apologists**. In 1945, a collection of ancient manuscripts, which included several Gnostic writings, was discovered near Nag Hammadi, Egypt. A popular text from the discovery is the Gospel of Thomas, a compilation of 114 sayings of Jesus some of which are also in the Synoptic Gospels. The Nag Hammadi library allowed scholars to study Gnosticism based on the Gnostics own writings rather than those of their opponents. It also revealed that there were Jewish, Christian and Pagan Gnostics.[12] In her book, *What is Gnosticism*, Karen King points out that term wasn't used until the seventeenth century, and in the twenty-first century it is still a complex topic. Although the Nag Hammadi library revealed that the Gnostics' beliefs and teachings were extremely diverse, much about the individual groups that authored the writings remains a mystery. There is also the assertion that rather than being a heretical offshoot of the Proto-Orthodox, what became orthodox Christianity was in fact a byproduct of Gnosticism.[13]

Ultimately, the Proto- Orthodox won the theological debate about Jesus. To a great extent, they owe their victory to the Roman Emperor

Constantine. Around the year 311 or 312, he became their champion rather than persecutor. It is still debated whether he truly converted to Christianity, but he did attribute his success in a crucial battle to divine intervention from the God of the Christians. Following that event, he began to support the Proto-Orthodox. He built churches, made bishops state officials by putting them on the government's payroll, and also built them homes. More importantly, he actively participated in the groups' administrative and theological concerns. In 321, he instituted the observance of Sunday as a day of rest throughout the Roman Empire. At the time, the Proto-Orthodox were observing the Sabbath as the day of rest on Saturday, and commemorating Jesus' resurrection on Sunday.[14] In June of 325, Constantine convened the Council of Nicaea to address the ongoing dispute about the nature of Jesus: whether he was fully divine and therefore of the same substance as God, or not. The dispute is known as the Arian controversy in reference to Arius the Alexandrian priest who was the chief proponent of the view that Jesus was not of the same substance as God. The matter was resolved by the adoption of the Nicene Creed. After the Council of Nicaea, Constantine issued an Edict against Heretics which forbade such groups from meeting, closed their places of worship, and ordered the destruction of their books.[15] Of course, those considered heretics were the theological rivals of the Proto-Orthodox.

The theology of the Proto- Orthodox came to represent Christianity. When creating the New Testament, they systematically chose writings that reinforced their views and discredited those of their rivals. One method they employed was to include books with different viewpoints about Jesus. For example, the Synoptic Gospels which portray Jesus as fully human, and the Gospel of John which portrays him in part as divine. This tactic supported the Proto-Orthodox position that Jesus was both human and divine, and discredited their opponents' who maintained that he was either fully human or fully divine. Another consequential choice was the inclusion of books that promoted the subordination of women and the exclusion of those that allowed women to teach and lead independently.[16] Two thousand plus years later, women throughout Western society, and particularly some aspiring clergy, have not fully recover from that decision.

*Apostolic Fathers – Second century Proto-Orthodox theologians and authors.
*Apology – From Greek word for defense, a reasoned explanation of one's beliefs and customs.

Historical Context of Second Temple Judaism

The Synoptic Gospels and other New Testament texts were written by first century Jewish groups during the Second Temple period. Thus they are among the writings categorized as Second Temple Jewish literature, even if they are not always included in comprehensive studies of those texts. The Second Temple period began around 539 BCE when the Persians conquered the Babylonians and became the ruling power in the ancient Near East. It officially ended in 135 CE when the Romans crushed the Bar Kokhba revolt at Bethar. Although the temple was destroyed in 70 CE, rebellion against Roman occupation of Judea continued until this final defeat. As a further punishment, the Romans changed the name of the land of Israel to Palestine or *Palestinia* meaning land of the Philistines.[17]

Scholars separate the Second Temple period into four eras. The Persian era lasted approximately two hundred years, from 539 – 332 BCE. It was followed by the Hellenistic era which began in 332 BCE with the triumphs of Alexander the Great. It ended in 63 BCE with the Romans' conquest of Judea. During the Hellenistic era, there was a third era that of the **Maccabean** or **Hasmonean**. When Alexander died in 322 BCE his empire was divided among four of his generals, and Judea remained subject to foreign rule. In 167 BCE, it was ruled by the Syrian king Antiochus IV Epiphanes who banned Jewish customs and practices including Sabbath worship. He also looted the temple and placed a statute of Zeus in it. The Maccabees led the military resistance against Antiochus's policies. In 164 BCE they defeated the Syrians and successfully regained control of the temple. The holiday of Hanukah commemorates this momentous event. Under the Maccabees, Judea remained independent for roughly one hundred years until the Roman era began in 63 BCE.[18]

This is an appropriate point to consider the terms Judaism, Jewish and Jew. In modern times, these words are associated with Judaism as one of the world's religions. In the ancient world, they simply referred to persons from or of Judea. After the Babylonian exile the Israelites were called Judeans or Jews: Yehuda in Hebrew; *Ioudaios* in Greek; *Iudaeus* in Latin.[19] This was a geographical and not religious designation. Although Pamela Eisenbaum explains that among the **diaspora** of the first century, Jews no longer limited their self-definition to geography or genealogy, but added the Greek concept of a common *politeia*, meaning constitution and way of life. **Philo** and **Josephus** were two prominent first century Jews whose writings reflect this concept of Judaic identity.[20] Philo was the philosopher from Alexander, Egypt who used Greek philosophy to interpret the Hebrew scriptures. Josephus was the Jewish historian who not only espoused the concept of the Torah as the Jewish *politeia*, constitution, but also maintained that Judaism was a philosophy comparable to or even superior to other ancient philosophies.[21]

As first century Jewish authors Philo and Josephus share the New Testament authors' historical context of Second Temple Judaism and the Greco-Roman world. Josephus is especially relevant to the study of the Synoptic Gospels and the New Testament because his writings are the primary source of information about first century Israel or Palestine. Josephus was born in Jerusalem in 35 CE and died in Rome around the year 100. He says his ancestors were priests and Hasmoneans. When he was sixteen he affiliated with each of the major first century Jewish groups: the Pharisees, the Sadducees, and the Essenes. Ultimately, he decided to become a disciple of a teacher named Banus and remained with him for three years. During the war that resulted in the destruction of Jerusalem, he was made a military commander in Galilee. When he and his troops were surrounded by Roman soldiers, they agreed to commit suicide rather than surrender. Josephus and one other man were the final survivors and rather than committing suicide they surrendered to the Roman general Vespasian. Josephus wisely prophesied to Vespasian that he would become the Roman emperor, which occurred when the Emperor Nero died in 68 CE.[22] After the war, Josephus went to Rome and served in Vespasian's court as a historian. He also changed his name to Vespasian's family name Flavius. Over the next twenty-five years he wrote four books in Greek about the Jewish people: *Jewish Wars*, which Ehrman says has six volumes and Steve Mason seven; *Jewish Antiquities*, a twenty volume history of the Jewish people from Adam to Josephus' time; *Against Apion*, a two volume Jewish apology; *Life*, his autobiography.[23]

Along with the writings of Philo and Josephus, another type of Second Temple writings are the **Apocrypha,** from a Greek word meaning hidden or secret. The Apocrypha are fourteen books of multiple genres that were written during the Hellenistic era of the Second Temple period. The names with the approximate dates for the composition of the books are:

Tobit – 225 -175 BCE.

Judith – 100 BCE.

Esther – 115 BCE.

Wisdom of Solomon – 50 BCE.

Sirach or Ecclesiasticus – 200-175 BCE.

Baruch – 200-100 BCE.

Prayer of Azariah and Song of the Three Holy Children – 1st century BCE.

Story of Susanna – 333- 160 BCE.

Bel and the Dragon – 200 -100 BCE.

Prayer of Manasseh – 1st or 2nd century BCE.

1Maccabees – 100 BCE.

2Maccabees – 150-100 BCE.

1Esdras 2nd century BCE.

2Esdras – 70-218 CE. [24]

The Apocrypha were not in the Hebrew Bible, but were added to its Greek translation the **Septuagint**. Scribes began translating the Hebrew Bible into Greek in 275 BCE at Alexandria, Egypt to accommodate

Greek speaking Jews in the diaspora. Contrary to the legend of its simultaneous creation by seventy-two scribes in seventy - two days, it actually took approximately two hundred years to fully complete the project.[25]

The Septuagint was not an exact translation of the Hebrew scriptures. In addition to inserting the Apocrypha, it was arranged differently. The Hebrew Bible is organized around three sections: Torah (the first five books), Prophets (*Nevi'im*) and Writings (*Ketuvim*) - thus the acronym for the Hebrew scriptures Tanakh. The Septuagint had four sections: Law, History, Poetry, and Prophets. While the Writings are the last section in the Hebrew Bible, the Prophets were the last section in the Septuagint. Consequently, the book of Chronicles is the last book in the Hebrew Bible and the book of Malachi the last book in the Septuagint and its many subsequent translations which includes the Old Testament section of the 1611 King James Bible. Originally, the King James Bible included the Apocrypha between the Old Testament and the New Testament. They were removed early in the 1800s, but remain in other Christian Bibles, notably the Catholic, the Greek Orthodox, and some other Protestant versions. *Mind The Gap* highlights the fact that there is a four hundred year gap between the date of the composition of the last book of the Old Testament, Malachi and the first book of the New Testament, the Gospel of Matthew. Furthermore, writings like the Apocrypha that were penned during the latter half of that gap are not only closer in time, but in many instances thought, to the New Testament texts.

This similarly applies to the Second Temple writings known as the **Pseudepigrapha**, from a Greek term meaning false writing. Pseudepigraphy, composing texts in the name of an admired or historical person, was a common ancient literary technique. As it pertains to biblical studies, Henze defines them as ancient Jewish and Christian writings that are not in the Old Testament, the Septuagint or the New Testament. Many of the Jewish pseudepigrapha are attributed to ancient biblical characters such as, for example, Enoch, Abraham, and Moses. These writings were in circulation well before the canonization of the Hebrew Bible was finalized in the second century CE. One reason they were excluded from the Hebrew Bible is that they were written after the Persian period and so thought too recent for inclusion in the canon.[26]

Other crucial Second Temple writings are the **Dead Sea Scrolls**. Some of the scrolls were discovered accidentally in 1947 in a cave near Jericho. Over the next nine years, manuscripts were found in eleven caves near Qumran along the Dead Sea. Approximately nine hundred texts of various genres were recovered, many only in fragments. Archeologists determined that the scrolls belonged to the **Essenes**. The scrolls consisted of writings specific to the community's beliefs and practices that were written between the second century BCE and first century CE. The collection included copies of the Hebrew Bible, minus the book of Esther, and their copies were one thousand years older than those in existence. The scrolls also contained Hebrew or Aramaic copies of some of the Apocrypha and the Pseudepigrapha.[27]

Although there are no references to the Essenes in the New Testament, long before the Dead Sea Scrolls were discovered, historians knew of them from the writings of the Roman author Pliny the Elder, as well as Josephus and Philo. The group emerged during the era of the Maccabees. They formed their monastic community around 150 BCE in protest against the Maccabees' appointment of a non-Zadokite as High Priest, and in anticipation of the final battle that would inaugurate God's earthly kingdom. It is thought that they hid their writings at Qumran during the war that led to the destruction of the Temple in 70 CE.[28]

The Dead Sea Scrolls gave scholars another window into the Second Temple period and first century Judaism. They disclosed that the Essenes were a prophetic community.[29] This affirmed that the spirit of prophecy continued among ordinary Second Temple Jews, including the first century followers of Jesus, despite the assertion of elites like the Pharisees that prophecy had ceased.[30] The 2000 discovery of the *Gabriel Revelation*, a first century BCE or first century CE Jewish apocalyptic writing, further documented the presence of prophecy.[31] According to Samuel Sandmel, Philo also maintained that prophecy had not ended.[32] Josephus appeared to reconcile the view that prophecy had ended and the evidence that prophecy continued by distinguishing between the end of prophecy and the end of the succession of the prophets.[33]

Like the Essenes, the other known major first century Jewish groups, the **Pharisees, Sadducees**, and **Fourth Philosophy** emerged during the era of the Maccabees. Of the estimated four million Jews living in the Roman Empire in the first century, most did not belong to one of these groups. The Essenes had around 4,000 members, the Pharisees 6,000 and the Sadducees and Fourth Philosophy each had less. The Pharisees meticulously observed both the written and developing oral law that was later codified in the Talmud. Their name may come from a Persian word meaning separated ones. They emphasized rules of ritual purity and most were laymen not priest. During the time of Jesus they tended to gather at the synagogues in Palestine rather than the temple.[34] They were the only first century Jewish group to survive after the destruction of the temple, and eventually became the principle representative of Judaism. The Sadducees were the first century Jewish aristocracy. Most were priest at the temple in Jerusalem. They were the majority members of the **Sanhedrin**, the council that oversaw all aspects of Jewish religious and civic affairs and served as the political liaison between the Jews and the Roman governor of Palestine. The Sadducees strictly followed the written torah. They did not share the Pharisees' observance of the oral law or their belief in resurrection. They disappeared after the destruction of the temple and left no writings. The groups that Josephus called the Fourth Philosophy violently resisted the Romans. The **Sicarii** were a mid-first century group who kidnapped and assassinated Jewish officials who cooperated with the Romans. The **Zealots** were a later first century group who went to Jerusalem from Galilee around 67 CE and overthrew the Sadducees. Their actions ultimately led to the Romans' destruction of Jerusalem and the temple.[35]

The six hundred year Second Temple period, especially the Hellenistic Era, along with the first century Greco-Roman world provide the historical background for the study of the Synoptic Gospels and the New Testament. The Septuagint was created during this period. It was the Septuagint that Greek speaking Jews read, and the New Testament authors quoted in their books. Their texts appropriately reflect both their Judaic roots and the Greco-Roman world.

Historical Context of the Greco-Roman World[36]

The expression Greco-Roman world refers to the geographical area and culture around the Mediterranean from the time of Alexander to the time of Constantine in the fourth century. As king of Macedonia, Alexander expanded his empire by conquering vast territories such as Egypt, Persia, and extending as far east as India. He then consolidated his empire by requiring all of the countries subject to his authority to adopt the Greek language, culture, and cultic rituals. He also built Greek cities in the conquered territories with Greek theaters, gymnasiums, and public baths. The technical name for this process is **Hellenization**, from *Hellas*, the Greek word for Greece. The phrase Greco-Roman also describes the cultural unity that occurred when the Romans retained Alexander's Hellenization program. The Romans promoted the use of the Greek language, Greek culture, and the worship of the Greek gods along with the Roman gods throughout the Roman empire.

Most people in the Greco-Roman world, other than the Jews, practiced polytheism. **Pagan** and **Gentile** were not derogatory terms. In fact, the word pagan did not exist. The first record of its use is from the fourth century where it referred to non- Christians - people who were not baptized. Later historians applied the term paganism to the cultic practices of the polytheistic religions.[37] Gentile, a term that appears throughout the New Testament, was a person who was not a Jew whether Christian or pagan.

Because pagans believed that the gods were involved in the day to day affairs of their lives, they focused on the present life not the afterlife, and cultic rituals rather than doctrines or creeds. Ehrman uses the visual of a pyramid to explain the hierarchy of divine beings in the Greco-Roman world. At the top of the pyramid was the one god, the Greek god Zeus, or the Roman god Jupiter. For some philosophers, like the Pre-Socratic Xenophanes, the Neoplatonists and Neopythagoreans a powerful unknowable God occupied this highest level. At the next level were the **daimonia** and the local gods. The English word demon is related to this Greek word daimonia, but in the Greco- Roman context it did not have a negative connation. It is defined as a category of divine beings that were less powerful than the gods, far more powerful than humans, and capable of influencing human lives. People employed cultic acts to cause the daimonia to behave in a beneficial rather than harmful manner. The local gods were individual household and family gods. At the lowest level were the demigods. Demigods were individuals born from the union of a god or goddess and a human being. They also were humans that came to be considered divine such as the emperor or people like the pagan philosopher, healer, and teacher **Apollonius of Tyanna**. He lived during the time of Jesus, is said to have performed miracles, and was considered a son of God. So within the context of the Greco-Roman world accounts like those the Gospels convey of Jesus, a wise teacher who performed miracles and was called a son of God were not unusual.

The polytheistic cults did not address issues of **cosmogony**, **cosmology** or **morality**. Topics of this kind were the subject of the philosophical schools, the mystery cults and the various Jewish groups. The major philosophical schools of the first century Greco-Roman world were **Stoicism**, **Epicureanism** and **Platonism**. Although Platonism was no longer an active school in the first century, it continued to influence other philosophical groups as well as the subsequent Apostolic Fathers. Plato was the fourth century BCE Greek philosopher who taught that the physical world, the world experienced by virtue of the physical senses, was merely a copy of the real invisible world, the world of eternal forms that human beings could come to know through the use of reason. Epicureanism encouraged reliance on the senses and the enjoyment of sensual pleasures such as food and drink. They believed that the gods had no interests in the lives of humans so it was unnecessary to worship or fear them.[38] The most important philosophical movement in the first century was Stoicism. It encouraged its followers to understand the way the world worked and to live in harmony with it without allowing anything outside of themselves to affect their well-being. Their goal was to live in accordance with nature free of passion or emotion.[39] You will recall that Josephus considered Judaism a philosophy and he equated the major first century Jewish groups to major philosophical schools. He likened the Pharisees to the Stoics, the Essenes to the Pythagoreans, and the Sadducees to the Epicureans.[40] All of the philosophical schools were exclusive groups that actively recruited converts, stressed the primacy of reason, and the need for education and discipline. A person could participate in several polytheistic cults and mystery schools at the same time, but not more than one philosophical school. Though a person could be a pagan priest and a member of one of the philosophical groups.

A central feature of the Greco- Roman world was the mystery cult. Here again, in the Greco-Roman world, the word cult was not offensive. The term comes from a Latin phrase, *cultus deorum*, meaning care for the gods. Mystery cults were groups that utilized initiation rituals and cultic practices to impact their members' earthly lives and life after death. They were located throughout the Mediterranean, in Greece, Persia, Egypt, and Syria. Each mystery cult had its own secret customs and rituals. Their common element was a myth involving the death and rebirth of a god or goddess linked to the annual vegetation cycle of winter and spring.

There are those who claim that Christianity, "the Jesus movement," also was a mystery cult and what the New Testament Gospels relate as history, initially was understood as myth. In Ehrman's opinion, there is not sufficient knowledge about the practices of the mystery cults, since they were secret societies, to definitively explain the relation between them and Christianity. He suggests that the more appropriate question is whether Gentile outsiders would have viewed Christianity as a kind of mystery cult analogous to those they knew. On the other hand,

Samuel Sandmel saw a clear resemblance between Paul's Christology and the mystery religions and maintained that Paul's Gentile audience would have immediately recognized the similarity. Sandmel defined the mystery religions as ancient cults which utilized rites and ceremonies, offered philosophical explanations of the ceremonies, and gave the initiate his salvation from the world and death.[41] In addition to the Pagan cults, there were also secret Jewish groups during the Second Temple period, one example being the Essenes as indicated in their writings.

Some other important aspects of the Greco- Roman world: It was an oral society. Most people could not read or write. It had a high mortality rate as there were no cures for most diseases. It was a hierarchical society. The majority of the population were poor and subordinate to a small wealthy upper class. The poor were mainly small farmers, serfs on large estates and in urban areas crafts men. It was a slave society. Approximately one third of the people in urban areas were slaves. One wealthy Roman could own as many as two thousand slaves. On the issue of slavery, Raymond Brown said, the huge Roman estates needed an abundance of slaves to manage them. And yet the status of slaves varied. Those who rowed in galleys or worked in the quarries had a brutal existence… but slaves also had legal rights, and under the empire abusing or killing slaves constituted a punishable crime. Besides working in business, farming, and households, slaves could be administrators, physicians, teachers, scholars, poets, and accumulate wealth.[42] Finally, the Greco-Roman world was a highly patriarchal society. Fathers had supreme authority over their households, which included their immediate and extended families, and servants. Fathers decided if a child, whether born to his wife or a slave, would be raised within the household, put up for adoption, sold, or left to die by exposure. Fathers had the authority to sell a child into slavery, allow or refuse the right to marriage or divorce, and retain any property of a child as their own. Their authority continued as long as they lived.[43]

This is a brief summary of the historical context of the Greco-Roman world. Before turning to the Synoptic Gospels, we should address two additional issues. First, the application of the word religion to the ancient polytheistic cults, the mystery schools, and in the previous section, the Gnostic groups. The word religion is based on the Latin *religio* from the verb *leig* meaning to bind. Originally, it was associated with the performance of cultic rituals. By the fourth century it was used to define the bond between humans and the gods, and in the fifth century Augustine used it to define the relation between believers and God.[44] There was no word in biblical Hebrew or ancient Greek for religion. Although modern writers refer to these ancient groups as ancient religions, that is not how they would have identified themselves because the word religion did not exist before the fourth century. Second, the reality that the question myth or history pervades the biblical writings, Old and New testaments. As such, the ultimate interpretive question may not be whether a story is historically factual, but what eternal truth does the story or passages present?

***Cosmogony**- Theories about the origin of the universe.
***Cosmology** – Theories about the structure of the universe.
***Morality** – Theories about right and wrong.

The Gospel of Mark

The Synoptic Gospels are the first three books in the New Testament. Originally, they did not include the titles now associated with them: Matthew, Mark and Luke. These were added in the second century by one of the Apostolic Fathers. They are called the Synoptic Gospels because they tell many of the same stories yet are distinct compositions. Synoptic is a combination of two Greek and Latin words meaning seen together. Each Gospel was written in the first century: Mark between 65 and 70; Matthew and Luke between 80 and 85. Each was written in Greek by a different unknown author at different locations outside of Palestine. Although the New Testament begins with the Synoptic Gospels, they are not the oldest New Testament writings. The earliest are Paul's seven surviving epistles: I Thessalonians, Romans, I and II Corinthians, Galatians, Phillipi, and Philemon. Paul wrote his letters between 49 and 62 CE, with I Thessalonians being the earliest of the New Testament's twenty-seven texts.

The **Synoptic Problem** is the phrase New Testament scholars invented to address the fact that the Synoptic Gospels have significant differences and tell similar stories. The **Four-Source Hypothesis** is the theory scholars developed to resolve the problem. According to the Four-Source theory, Mark was written first and independently used by the authors of Matthew and Luke to write their Gospels. The authors of Matthew and Luke used an additional source called **Q**, from the

German word *Quelle* meaning source, for stories in their Gospels that are not in Mark. Matthew had a source, called **M,** for material that is only in in the Gospel of Matthew, and Luke a source called **L** for stories that are only in the Gospel of Luke.

The word gospel is from the Greek word *evangelion* meaning good news or proclamation. When capitalized, Gospel is a literary genre that narrates stories about Jesus. There were many of these writings when the New Testament was created, but it only includes four: the Synoptic Gospels and the Gospel of John. The other New Testament genres are the Epistles, a General History- Acts and one **Apocalypse** -Revelation. Each of the New Testament genres has its own literary features and may contain subgenres or literary forms. The Gospels are the genre. The parables within the Gospels, for example, are literary forms. We generally define a parable as an earthly story with a heavenly meaning. A more formal definition is a self-contained short story with a moral message. Parables differ from allegories where the content of the story is symbolic of a larger principle or idea.[45]

The genre apocalypse is related to the term **apocalypticism** and its adjective **apocalyptic**. Apocalypse is a Greek word meaning unveiling, revealing or revelation. Even though themes of apocalypticism are present in some of the Hebrew Bible prophetic books, it was primarily a late Second Temple belief that the present age was controlled by evil forces that would soon be destroyed. Apocalypticism is one type of eschatology, from the Greek word *Eschaton* meaning last, and referring to theories about the end of time or lasts days. There are various notions about eschatology. For some, it means the destruction of the material universe. For others it means the end of the existing world order and its injustices. Others envision it as the time when God will transform the physical world to free it of disease and disasters. Still others believe the last days means social, political and religious transformation resulting in everyone living in accordance with God's will.[46] As a type of eschatology, apocalypticism describes the state of the world just prior to the last days, and the imminent expectation that God would send his deliverer to vindicate his people and establish his kingdom.

As literary genres the Gospels are ancient biographies. The ancient biography was not identical to the modern biography. Modern biographies seek to convey factually accurate information about their subjects. Ancient biographies sought to demonstrate the virtue and character of their subjects rather than relay actual events or historical facts. Ancient biographies, like the modern biography, were usually based on oral and written sources, but their primary objective was to describe their subject's character based on their words, deeds and human interactions. Ancient biographies did not include character development of their subjects because ancient people believed that character remained the same throughout a person's life. Typically, the ancient biography began by stating the subject's identity and character.

Accordingly, each Synoptic Gospels begins by conveying a particular interpretation of Jesus based on the respective tradition of the author. A **tradition** within the context of this study is any doctrine, idea, practice, or custom that has been handed down from one person to another. The Gospel of Mark opens with the sentence, "The beginning of the gospel of Jesus Christ, the son of God." This opening introduces Jesus first, as the Christ, and second, as the son of God. The word Christ is the English translation of the Greek word *christos,* which was the Greek translation of the Hebrew word for messiah. Both terms mean the anointed one. In the Hebrew Bible, the verb *masch* is used in connection with the anointing of kings, prophets, and priests. It is not used to designate the future deliverer associated with apocalypticism and the end of days. It was during the period of Second Temple Judaism that apocalyptic writers began to interpret certain Hebrew Bible scriptures as promising a future Messiah for Israel.[47]

There were different ideas about the expected Messiah. In light of God's promise to give David an everlasting kingdom, some thought the Messiah would be a descendant of David and warrior king. In light of the language in Daniel 7:13, others thought the Messiah would be a cosmic judge. The Essenes envisioned two Messiahs, a Davidic or royal Messiah and a priestly Messiah, as well as an eschatological prophet.[48] Thus re-creating the prophet, priest and king scenario of ancient Israel. The appellation son of man is relevant to the messiah concept. It appears over sixty times in the Synoptic Gospels, and other than in the Gospel of John, it is only used once in Acts and twice in Revelation. In first century Judaism "son of man" was an Aramaic phrase used as a synonym for man by a speaker to refer to himself. In the Synoptic Gospels it is only used by Jesus.[49] In the Hebrew Bible "son of man" meant a human male, and in Daniel 7 collectively the saints of the most High. In the pseudepigrapha text of I Enoch son of man explicitly refers to the expected Messiah. Overtime, the Daniel 7 son of man came to be interpreted as a reference to the Messiah. Ehrman and Vermes appear to propose that the authors of the Synoptic Gospels employed the son of man language to support their belief that Jesus was the Messiah. In any event, as an ancient biography, the Gospel of Mark begins by identifying Jesus as the Jewish Messiah. In the first century, this was a Jewish concept well known to Jews but not Gentiles.[50]

The second part of the introduction, the **son of God**, was familiar to first century Jews and Gentiles. In the Greco-Roman culture, sons of God were humans that came to be thought of as divine because of their miraculous deeds or inspirational teaching such as Apollonius of Tyanna and demigods. In Jewish culture, **Honi the Circle drawer** and **Hanina ben Dosa** were examples of men known as miracle workers and sons of God. Honi the circle drawer was a first century BCE Galilean who drew a circle around himself and promised not to leave it until God answered his prayer for rain. Hanina ben Dosa was a first century CE Galilean healer and miracle worker. In the Hebrew Bible kings, angels, and Israel are called God 's son. Some of the Apocrypha refer to the just man as God's son. Son of God was both a Jewish and Gentile title. Gentiles would have associated it with a miracle worker, inspirational teacher or demigod. Jews would have thought an angelic or celestial being, or saintly man.[51]

The author of the Gospel of Mark immediately follows his introduction of Jesus with the story of his baptism by John the Baptist. Each of the Synoptic Gospels tell the story of Jesus going from Galilee to Judea to be baptized by John. Each concludes the occurrence with a voice from heaven proclaiming this is my beloved son in whom I am well pleased. Josephus also reports of John performing baptisms. He was baptizing Jews not Gentiles. Scholars describe John the Baptist as an apocalyptic prophet who was preaching repentance and baptism in preparation for the kingdom of God and imminent end of the world. It is noteworthy that the Dead Sea Scrolls and some Apocrypha and Pseudepigrapha books indicate that other Jewish groups also practiced baptism before the followers of Jesus adopted it as a ritual of conversion to their communities.[52]

The Gospel of Mark probably was written during the early phase of the four year war that resulted in the destruction of the temple. It was written to a Jewish community outside of Palestine consisting of pagans that had converted to the Jesus Movement. The writing provides a chronological account of Jesus' public ministry beginning with his baptism and ending with his arrest, trial, crucifixion and ascension.

Structurally, it can be divided into four sections: chapter 1 verses 1-15, the introduction identifying Jesus as the Christ and son of God; chapter 1 verse 16 to chapter 8 verse 26, stories of him performing miracles, healings and teaching; chapter 8 verse 27 through chapter 15 verse 41, the **Passion,** suffering, narrative depicting Jesus' last days and crucifixion; chapter 16 verses 1 through 8, his resurrection. Originally, the book ended at verse 8. At some point a copyist added the remaining twelve verses.

Original Ending Mark 16: 1, 5-8

And when the sabbath was past, Mary Magdalene, and Mary the mother of James and Salome, had bought sweet spices, that they might come and anoint him.

And entering into the sepulcher, they saw a young man sitting on the right side, clothed in a long white garment, and they were affrighted.

And he saith unto them, Be not affrighted, ye seek Jesus of Nazareth, which was crucified, he is risen; he is not here, behold the place where they laid him.

But go your way, tell his disciples and Peter that he goeth before you into Galilee, there shall ye see him, as he said unto you.

And they went out quickly, and fled from the sepulcher, for they trembled and were amazed, neither said they anything to any man, for they were afraid.

Revised Ending Mark 16: 9-11; 19-20.

Now when Jesus was risen early the first day of the week, he appeared first to Mary Magdalene, out of whom he had cast seven devils.

And she went and told them that had been with him, as they mourned and wept.

And they, when they had heard that he was alive, and had been seen of her, believed not.

So then after the Lord had spoken unto them, he was received up into heaven and sat on the right hand of God.

And they went forth and preached everywhere, the Lord working with them, and confirming the word with signs following. Amen.

The major theme of the Gospel of Mark is that Jesus was crucified because he was the Messiah sent by God to die as a sacrifice for humanity. This message is communicated in the Passion narrative where his crucifixion is linked to the simultaneous tearing of the curtain of the Holy of Holies in the temple. This was an allusion to Yom Kippur the only day the High Priest entered the Holy of Holies to pray for the forgiveness of the sins of the children of Israel. The tearing of the veil is followed by a pagan soldier's acknowledgement of Jesus as the son of God. Mark 15:37-39: And Jesus cried with a loud voice, and gave up the ghost. And the veil of the temple was rent in twain from the top to the bottom. And when the centurion, which stood over against him, saw that he so cried out, and gave up the ghost, he said, truly this man was the son of God. For the author of the Gospel of Mark, Jesus was crucified because that was his divine purpose as the Christ and son of God.

The Gospel of Matthew

The Gospel of Matthew is the first book in the New Testament because when it was created theologians believed that Matthew was the earliest of the Synoptic Gospels. In the nineteenth century, modern historical methods revealed that Mark was most likely the oldest Synoptic Gospel. Scholars who perform this type of analysis work with the writings in Greek. They offer three primary reasons to support the conclusion that Mark was the first Gospel and two decades or so later the authors of the Gospels of Matthew and Luke used it in writing their Gospels.

First the patterns of agreement. Sometimes Matthew and Mark have the same wording for a story and Luke a different one. Other times Luke and Mark have the same wording and Matthew a different one. Rarely do Matthew and Luke have the same wording of a story found in Mark and Mark a different wording. These patterns of agreement, or wording, suggests that the authors of Matthew and Luke used the Gospel of Mark as one of their sources and made their own edits to it as in the accounts of Jesus' baptism by John.

Second the sequence of the narratives. Matthew and Luke basically agree in the wording of stories that are not found in Mark, such as the Disciples' prayer and the Beatitudes. They also placed those stories at different locations in their Gospels. In Matthew these verses are in the block of teaching known as the Sermon on the Mount. In Luke they are interspersed among other stories and teaching. Stories that are in each of the Synoptic Gospels, such as Jesus' baptism, appear in the same order, in the Gospels of Matthew and Luke, both in chapter three in the King James Bible. This sequence of the writings indicates that the authors of the Gospels of Matthew and Luke used Mark and some other source – Q which they inserted at different points in their Gospels.

Two other reasons given to support the finding that Mark is the earliest Gospel and was used as a source for the Gospels of Matthew and Luke are that the Gospels of Matthew and Luke grammatically and aesthetically are better writings. Lastly, Mark is the shortest of the Synoptics further indicating that it was written first.

Unlike the Gospel of Mark which begins by identifying Jesus as the Christ and son of God, the Gospel of Matthew begins by identifying Jesus as the Christ and the son of David and Abraham. Mathew 1:1, "The book of the generation of Jesus Christ, the son of David, the son of Abraham." These opening words are followed by a genealogy and birth narrative designed to demonstrate that Jesus was the anticipated Messiah who was expected to be a descendant of David. The genealogy is not historically accurate, but is manipulated to show that every fourteen generations a significant event occurs in the history of the Israelites, and that the birth of Jesus was the significant event of that time. The pattern of every fourteen years was likely used for symbolic reasons because fourteen is the numerical value of the name of David in Hebrew.

The Gospel of Matthew was written for a community comprised of Jews and Gentile converts located in an urban area close to Palestine. One of its unique features is its eleven **fulfillment citations**, a literary device that claims something experienced or done by Jesus fulfilled the words of a Hebrew Bible prophet. For example, Jesus' birth in Bethlehem fulfilled the Hebrew Bibles's prediction about where the Messiah would be born. Micah 5:2 is one of the scriptures that had come to be interpreted as referring to the Messiah. "But thou, Bethlehem Ephratah, though thou be little among the thousands of Judah, yet out of thee shall he come forth unto me that is to be ruler in Israel…" Jesus' parents taking him to Egypt to escape Herod's order to slaughter Jewish male infants is seen as a prediction of what would happen when the Messiah arrived in fulfillment of Hosea 11:1, "out of Egypt have I called my son." Jesus going to Egypt also portrays him as a teacher and prophet like Moses, a new Moses as promised in Deuteronomy 18:15, "the Lord thy God will raise up unto thee a prophet from the midst of thee, of thy brethren, like unto me…" The Gospel of Matthew actually is structured around five sections of discourses by Jesus, symbolic of the five books of Moses: the sermon on the mount in chapters five through seven; instructions to his disciples in chapter ten; the series of parables while sitting by the seaside in chapter thirteen; additional instruction to his disciples in chapter eighteen; the lengthy discourse that begins at chapter twenty three and contains some of his harshest criticism of the Pharisees and Sadducees.

Conflict between Jesus and the Jewish leaders is more prominent in the Gospel of Matthew than in the Gospel of Mark. In Mark, few recognize Jesus as the Messiah. According to William Wrede's **Messianic Secret** the reason no one recognized Jesus as the Messiah in the Gospel of Mark was because he did not claim to be the Messiah. The stories that say Jesus told anyone who recognized him as Messiah not tell others was an after the fact tactic to explain that he never actually claimed to be the Messiah. On the other hand, throughout the Gospel of Matthew Jesus is recognized as the Messiah and engages in continuous confrontations with the Jewish leaders.

He also teaches more on the Jewish law and the theme of righteousness. The first use of the word law in the New Testament is in Matthew 5:17, "think not that I am come to destroy the law or the prophets, I am not come to destroy but to fulfill." This is a clear reference to the first five books of the Hebrew Bible - *Torah*, and the prophetic books- *Nevi'im*. When Jewish scribes translated the Hebrew Bible into Greek, they translated *torah*, which meant teaching or instruction in Hebrew with the Greek word *nomos* which means law.[53] There is an obvious distinction between the Greek word for teaching *didache* and *nomos* - law. While the *Torah* does include specific laws, it is more books of teaching than rules of law. Whether law in a New Testament passage is referring to the *Torah*, in Greek, *Pentateuch* or some custom within the *Torah* is an interpretive question. In Mathew 5:17, it is of no real consequence whether Jesus is presented as saying I came not to destroy the law or the teaching, but to fulfill it. In either case, he does not disavow the *Torah* but stresses following it with a greater understanding of its true meaning and underlying purpose. This is seen in the six **Antitheses** in Matthew 5:21-48. Antitheses literally means contrary statement. In the Gospel of Matthew it represents six statements Jesus makes about the law followed by his interpretation.

Matthew 5: 21-22 Ye have heard that it was said by them of old time, Thou shalt not kill; and whosoever shall kill shall be in danger of the judgement. But I say unto you, that whosoever is angry with his brother without cause shall be in danger of the judgement: and whosoever shall say to his brother, Raca shall be in danger of the council, but whosoever shall say, thou fool, shall be in danger of hell fire.

Matthew 5:27 Ye have heard that it was said by them of old time, thou shall not commit adultery. But I say unto you, that whosoever looketh on a woman to lust after her hath committed adultery with her already in his heart.

Matthew 5: 31- 32 It hath been said, whosoever shall put away his wife, let him give her a writing of divorcement. But I say unto you, that whosoever shall put away his wife, saving for the cause of fornication, causeth her to commit adultery and whosoever shall marry her that is divorced committeth adultery.

Matthew 5:33-37 Again ye have heard that it hath been said by them of old time, thou shalt not forswear thyself, but shalt perform unto the Lord thine oaths. But I say unto you, swear not at all; neither by heaven for it is God's throne. Nor by the earth, for it is his footstool, neither by Jerusalem, for it is the city of the great king. Neither shalt thou swear by the head, because thou canst not make one hair white or black. But let your communication be, yea, yea, nay, nay, for whatsoever is more than these cometh of evil.

Matthew 5:38-39 Ye have heard that it hath been said, an eye for an eye and a tooth for a tooth. But I say unto you that ye resist not evil. But whosoever shall smite thee on thy right cheek, turn to him the other also.

Matthew 5:43-48 Ye have heard that it hath been said, thou shalt love thy neighbor, and hate thine enemy. But I say unto you, love your enemies, bless them that curse you, do good to them that hate you, and pray for them which despitefully use you and persecute you. That ye may be the children of your father which is in heaven. For he maketh his sun to rise on the evil and on the good and sendeth rain on the just and on the unjust. For if ye love them which love you, what reward have ye? Do not even the publicans the same? And if ye salute your brethren only, what do ye more than others? Do not even the publicans so? Be ye therefore perfect, even as your Father which is in heaven is perfect.

Perhaps the apex of Jesus' perception of the law is illustrated by his teaching on the great commandment. The story in the Gospel of Matthew is found at Mathew 22: 36-40. "Master which is the great commandment in the law? Jesus said unto him, thou shalt love the Lord thy God with all thy heart, and with all thy soul, and with all thy mind. This is the first and great commandment. And the second is like unto it, thou shalt love thy neighbor as thyself. On these two commandments hang all the law and the prophets." This teaching is in each Synoptic Gospel. In the Gospel of Mark it is at Mark 12:29-31. "And Jesus answered him, The first of all the commandments is, hear o Israel, the Lord our God is one Lord. And thou shalt love the Lord thy God with all thy heart, and with all thy soul, and with all thy mind, and with all thy strength, this is the first commandment. And the second is like, namely this, thou shalt love thy neighbor as thyself. There is none other commandment greater than these." The version in the Gospel of Luke is connected to the story of the good Samaritan. This teaching of love, love of God, love of neighbor and love of self as attributed to Jesus in the Synoptic Gospels is neither original nor unique.[54] Still, it is a sublime summation of the Judaic way of life. To the extent that members of Church of God and Saints of Christ, Temple Beth El, International Headquarters call these verses the Summary of the Commandments.

Martin Buber maintained that this command to love is not a feeling but an attitude.[55] To attitude, we must add act. An attitude and act of kindness toward others, and an attitude and acts of trust toward God. This love may not be mere feeling, but I suspect that many would insist that their love for God and the communities in which they learn to practice love of God and neighbor is accompany by a genuine and sacred feeling of love. Buber also says in his discussion of these scriptures that there is no concept of self- love in the Hebrew Bible. There is, however, a concept of self-love in Church of God and Saints of Christ, Temple Beth El, International Headquarters. One of our executive leaders, Rabbi Levi Solomon Plummer, taught, "take nothing at the expense of human dignity." This suggest that the mandate to love thy neighbor as thy self involves more than doing unto others as you would have them do unto you. It includes active care and concern for oneself. Not in a selfish or self-centered manner, but with the knowledge that just by virtue of being a human being, whether or not you are a person of faith, you merit the human courtesy of dignity and respect. Therefore we maintain that the essence of Church of God and Saints of Christ is love, love of God, love of others and love of self.

Another key feature of the Gospel of Matthew is the prayer found in chapter six verses nine through thirteen:

Our Father, which art in heaven, Hallowed be thy name. Thy kingdom come. Thy will be done in earth, as it is in heaven. Give us this day our daily bread. And forgive us our debts as we forgive our debtors. And lead us not into temptation, but deliver us from evil. For thine is the kingdom, and the power, and the glory, forever amen.

This prayer is known worldwide by Christians and non-Christians alike as the Lord's Prayer. In Luke chapter eleven verses one through four there is a similar version, without the closing, "for thine is the kingdom, and the power, and the glory, forever, amen." This close also is absent from the oldest copies of the Gospel of Matthew. It was added in the fourth century by a copyist who probably was familiar with *The Didache,* also known as *The Didache of the Twelve Apostles.* Didache as you know means teaching. *The Didache* is a composite text revised over time for a Jesus Movement community consisting of Jews and Gentiles. It originated in Palestine before the temple was destroyed in 70 CE.[56] It includes the Matthew version of the prayer and concludes, "For yours is the power and glory forever."[57] Scholars do not think that the either of these texts were used as a source for the other. Rather the writings imply that the communities for whom each writing was composed shared an earlier lost text or oral tradition. For centuries, *The Didache* was a popular and respected first century document. It was not on Athanasius 367 CE list of texts that should be classified as canon, but it was among the writings, including some of the Apocrypha, that he recommended in that letter as suitable for instruction.[58] *The Didache* disappeared in the fifth century, but was re-discovered in a monastery in 1893. In addition to the prayer which *The Didache* says should be recited three times a day, it contains some of the Gospel of Matthew's

Antithesis statements. Praying three times a day was an ancient Israelite practice as reflected in Psalm 55:17, "Evening, and morning, and at noon, will I pray..." The prayer itself resembles standard Jewish prayers such as the Kaddish.[59] This reinforces the Judaic origins of these first century writings, the Gospel of Matthew and *The Didache*. Members of Church of God and Saints of Christ, Temple Beth El, International Headquarters call the Matthew prayer the Disciples' Prayer and also recite it three times a day, at 6:00 PM, 6:00 AM and Noon. We should also mention that the pronouncement that the Congregation uses to bless meals taken from Revelation 7:12 is likewise of Judaic origin since the book of Revelation also is a first century Jewish text.[60]

The Gospel of Luke

The Gospel of Luke was written around the same time as the Gospel of Matthew by a Gentile convert for a community of Gentile converts to the first century Judaism about Jesus. Although it is an ancient biography, it does not follow the ancient biography openings of the Gospels of Mark and Matthew. Instead the Gospel of Luke opens with a preface typical of ancient histories. It is generally believed that the author of the Gospel of Luke also wrote the book of Acts, and the Gospels' initial verses were intended as the introduction to both works. Luke 1:1-4:

Forasmuch as many have taken in hand to set forth in order a declaration of those things which are most surely believed among us. Even as they delivered them unto us, which from the beginning were eyewitnesses, and ministers of the word.

It seemed good to me also, having had perfect understanding of all things from the very first, to write unto thee in order, most excellent Theophilus.

That thou mightiest know the certainty of those things, wherein thou hast been instructed.

There is a debate about the identity of Theophilus, whether it is the name of a Roman official, or a symbolic reference to the author's community. The name means lover of God or beloved of God.

The introduction is followed by birth narratives for John and Jesus. Luke 1:5, 11-17:

There was in the days of Herod, the king of Judea, a certain priest named Zacharias, of the course of Abia: and his wife was of the daughters of Aaron, and her name was Elisabeth.

And there appeared unto him an angel of the Lord standing on the right side of the altar of incense.

And when Zacharias saw him, he was troubled, and fear fell upon him.

But the angel said unto him, fear not, Zacharias, for thy prayer is heard, and thy wife, Elisabeth shall bear thee a son, and thou shalt call his name John.

And thou shalt have joy and gladness, and many shall rejoice at his birth.

For he shall be great in the sight of the Lord, and shall drink neither wine nor strong drink, and shall be filled with the Holy Ghost even from his mother's womb.

And many of the children of Israel shall he turn to the Lord their God.

And he shall go before him in the spirit and power of Elijah, to turn the hearts of the fathers to the children, and the disobedient to the wisdom of the just, to make ready a people prepared for the Lord.

John's birth narrative establishes his Judaic pedigree with its setting in the temple at Jerusalem where his father learns of his future birth while performing his priestly functions. The birth narrative for Jesus, as in the

Gospel of Matthew, describes his conception by the Holy Ghost, but also reveals that John and Jesus were cousins. Luke1:26-36:

And in the sixth month the angel Gabriel was sent from God unto a city of Galilee, named Nazareth,

To a virgin espoused to a man whose name was Joseph of the house of David, and the virgin's name was Mary.

And the angel came in unto her, and said, Hail, thou art highly favored, the Lord is with thee: blessed art thou among women.

And when she saw him, she was troubled at his saying, and cast in her mind what manner of salutation this should be.

And the angel said unto her, Fear not, Mary: for thou has found favor with God.

And behold, thou shalt conceive in thy womb, and bring forth a son, and shalt call his name Jesus.

He shall be great, and shall be called the Son of the Highest: and the Lord God shall give unto him the throne of his father David.

And he shall reign over the house of Jacob forever; and of his kingdom there shall be no end.

Then said Mary unto the angel, How shall this be, seeing I know not a man?

And the Angel answered and said unto her, the Holy Ghost shall come upon thee, and the power of the Highest shall overshadow thee, therefore also that holy thing which shall be born of thee shall be called the Son of God.

And behold, thy cousin Elisabeth, she hath also conceived a son in her old age: and this is the sixth month with her, who was called barren.

Luke is the only Gospel to indicate that John and Jesus were relatives with a lifelong connection that began when both were still in their mother's wombs. Luke 1:39-42:

And Mary arose in those days, and went into the hill country with haste, into a city of Juda.

And entered into the house of Zacharia, and saluted Elisabeth.

And it came to pass, that when Elisabeth heard the salutation of Mary, the babe leaped in her womb, and Elisabeth was filled with the Holy Ghost.

And she spake out with a loud voice, and said, Blessed art thou among women, and blessed is the fruit of thy womb.

Thus it may not have been a haphazard occurrence when Jesus goes to Judea as a grown man to be baptized by John as he is preaching repentance, baptizing and functioning, as foretold in his birth narrative, as a prophet in the spirit and power of Elijah. Like the other Synoptic Gospels, the author of the Gospel of Luke uses Malachi 4:5 and Isaiah 40:3 to depict John as the prophet Elijah "Behold I will send you Elijah the prophet before the coming of the great and dreadful day of the Lord;" "The voice of him that crieth in the wilderness, prepare ye the way of the Lord, make straight in the dessert a highway for God." That Elijah would precede the Messiah was a long held Judaic belief.

Jesus' genealogy follows his baptism. Unlike the Gospel of Matthew which opens with Jesus' ancestry beginning with Abraham and ending with Joseph, the husband of Mary. The genealogy in the Gospel of Luke starts with Joseph and ends with Adam, "which was the son of God." By tracing Jesus' ancestry back to Adam, Luke identifies Jesus as more than the Messiah and prophet to the Jewish people, but a prophet and savior for Gentiles as well.[61]

The Gospel of Luke is the only Synoptic Gospel that explicitly identifies Jesus as Messiah, prophet and savior. Luke 2:11, "For unto you is born this day in the city of David a savior, which is Christ the Lord." The Gospel of Mark identifies him as Christ and son of God. Son of God, as previously stated, was a Jewish and Greco- Roman expression. In Second Temple Judaism some miracle workers were called sons of God, and in the Hebrew Bible kings, angels, and Israel collectively were called sons of God. In Greco-Roman culture, sons of God were humans that came to be thought of as divine because of their miraculous deeds or inspirational teaching and demigods. The Gospel of Mark likewise portrays Jesus as a prophet. Mark 6:4, "But Jesus said unto them, a prophet is not without honor, but in his own country, and among his own kin, and in his own house." The Gospel of Matthew also portrays Jesus as Christ, prophet, and by implication in its birth narrative a son of God. These birth narratives in the Gospels of Matthew and Luke combine the Judaic concepts of Messiah and prophet with the Greco- Roman concept of demigod. You will recall that in the Greco- Roman world a demigod was a person born from the union of a god or goddess and a human being. Such birth stories were not uncommon. Even Pythagoras was said to be the offspring of the god Apollo and a virgin mother.[62] The birth narrative and the designation of the infant Jesus as savior would have invoked for the Gentile members of Luke's community this feature of Greco-Roman culture and its concept of salvation.

Today salvation is essentially a religious term related to a person's internal spiritual existence or state of consciousness. The word itself is the English translation of the Greek noun *soteria* and the Hebrew noun *yeshua*. Both words basically mean help, deliverance, rescue, victory, wellness. In the Greco-Roman world, the *soteria* sought in Pagans' day to day affairs was present life, physical, practical and external. This aspect of soteria was not unlike *yeshua* in the Hebrew Bible where God saved, delivered or rescued from some external, earthly situation or condition.[63]

Overtime, a picture of a Judaic end of days salvation emerged. One example is in Isaiah 2:2-4:

And it shall come to pass in the last days, that the mountain of the Lord's house shall be established in the top of the mountains, and shall be exalted above the hills, and all nations shall flow unto it.

And many people shall go and say, come ye, and let us go up to the mountain of the Lord, to the house of the God of Jacob, and he will teach us of his ways, and we will walk in his paths, for out of Zion shall go forth the law, and the word of the Lord from Jerusalem.

And he shall judge among the nations, and shall rebuke many people, and they shall beat their swords into plowshares, and their spears into pruning hooks, nation shall not lift up sword against nation, neither shall they learn war anymore.

During the Second Temple period, the concept of the Messiah and resurrection of the dead were added to Israel's eschatological expectation. A time of collective present life triumph, sovereignty and vindication for the nation and universal recognition of its God.

The Greco- Roman concept of salvation was personal rather than collective. This included the interior salvation offered in some of the philosophical schools and mystery cults.[64] Undeniably Judaism also has an individual internal element. An illustration is expressed in the scriptures that the King James Bible labels in the Gospels of Matthew and Mark as the Great Commandment, taken from Deuteronomy 6:5 and Leviticus 19:18. The Gospel of Luke also has this teaching. Luke 10:25-28:

And behold a certain lawyer stood up, and tempted him saying, Master what shall I do to inherit eternal life.

And he said unto him, what is written in the law? How readest thou?

And he answering said, thou shalt love the Lord thy God with all thy heart, and with all thy soul, and with all thy strength, and with all thy mind, and thy neighbor as thyself.

And he said unto him, thou hast answered right, this do, and thou shalt live.

Loving God, believing in God, and turning to God- repentance comprise the key elements of the Judaic inner life. While these factors have both individual and communal significance, Israel's expected eschatological salvation was for Israel collectively.

The Synoptic Gospels link Israel's collective eschatological salvation and Greco-Roman individual salvation. They describe Jesus preaching an apocalyptic eschatological message, the imminent realization of Israel's end of days vision - the kingdom of God, and offering access to the kingdom, individual salvation, for those who embrace his message.

The Gospel of Luke interprets the state of the kingdom of God and the means by which admission to it is obtained a bit differently than in the Gospels of Matthew and Mark. Those Gospels introduce Jesus' teaching as calling for repentance and announcing the imminent arrival of the kingdom. Mark 1:15, "And saying the time is fulfilled, and the kingdom of God is at hand, repent ye and believe the gospel." Matthew 4:17, "From that time Jesus began to preach and to say, repent for the kingdom of heaven is at hand." In those Gospels, the kingdom is generally imminent but still future. Mark 9:1, "And he said unto them, verily I say unto you, that there be some of them that stand here, which shall not taste of death till they have seen the kingdom of God come with power." Matthew 16: 28, "verily I say unto you, there be some standing here which shall not taste of death till they see the Son of man coming in his kingdom." Luke 9:27 also refers to the kingdom of God as future, "but I tell you of a truth, there be some standing here, which shall not taste of death till they see the kingdom of God." At the same time, the Gospel of Luke introduces Jesus as the present embodiment of the kingdom of God. It commences Jesus' teaching with him going to a synagogue on the sabbath day and reading from the book of the prophet Isaiah and its allusion to fiftieth year Jubilee in Leviticus 25. Luke 4:18-21:

The Spirit of the Lord is upon me, because he hath anointed me to preach the gospel to the poor, he hath sent me to heal the brokenhearted, to preach deliverance to the captives, and recovering of sight to the blind, to set at liberty them that are bruised.

To preach the acceptable year of the Lord.

And he closed the book, sand gave it to the minister and sat down. And the eyes of all them that were in the synagogue were fastened on him.

And he began to say unto them, this day is this scripture fulfilled in your ear.

Also, Luke 17: 21, "neither shall they say, lo here or lo there, for, behold, the kingdom of God is within you." We are told that the better translation of the phrase within you is among you. The kingdom of God as both present and future is characteristic of all of the Synoptic Gospels, the book of Acts and Paul's epistles.[65] One reason the kingdom of God as present is more noticeable in the Gospel of Luke is its central focus on the spread of the Jesus movement and the opportunity for the inclusion of Gentiles.

The Gospel of Luke's focus on the kingdom as present more than future is also seen in Jesus' concern about the social conditions of his time. For example, while Matthew begins the Beatitudes with Matthew 5:3, "Blessed are the poor in spirit, for theirs is the kingdom of heaven." Luke 5:20 speaks to those who are actually socially poor, "Blessed be ye poor for yours is the kingdom of God." The author includes women among those who travelled with Jesus. Luke 8:1-3: And it came to pass afterward, that he went throughout every city and village preaching and showing the glad tidings of the kingdom of God, and the twelve were with him.

And certain women, which had been healed of evil spirits and infirmities, Mary called Magdalene, out of whom went seven devils.

And Joanna the wife of Chuza Herod's steward, and Susanna, and many others, which ministered unto him of their substance.

(See also Mark 15:40-41). In Luke 10:48-42, Jesus commends Mary for choosing to sit at his feet to hear his teaching instead of joining her sister Martha with traditional women's work. This story is only in the Gospel of Luke reiterating the author's depiction of Jesus as the savior of the whole world including the socially oppressed.

Finally, the Gospel of Luke does not interpret Jesus' death as a vicarious atonement for sin like the Gospels of Mark and Matthew. In those writings this belief is symbolized by the simultaneous tearing of the curtain of the Holy of Holies at the moment of Jesus' death. Mark 15: 37- 38, "And Jesus cried with a loud voice, and gave up the ghost. And the veil of the temple was rent in twain from top to the bottom." Matthew 27: 50-51, "Jesus, when he had cried again with a loud voice yielded up the ghost. And behold, the veil of the temple was rent from the top to the bottom, and the earth did quake, and the rocks rent." These verses allude to the yearly observance of Yom Kippur, the only time when the High Priest entered the Holy of Holies to pray for atonement for the sins of Israel. In the Gospel of Luke the veil of the Holy of Holies tears before Jesus' death. Luke 23:45-46, "And the sun was darkened, and the veil of the temple was rent in the midst. And when Jesus had cried with a loud voice, he said, Father into thy hands I commend my spirit and having said thus, he gave up the ghost." Also the centurion in the Gospel of Luke says of Jesus, "certainly, this was a righteous man," while in the Gospels of Matthew and Mark he says truly he was the son of God. The author of the Gospel of Luke interprets Jesus death as that of an innocent martyr not a vicarious sacrifice. In this Gospel, it is not Jesus' death that brings salvation but the response to his call for repentance. In this regard, the Gospel of Luke's theory of salvation is in line with that of traditional Judaism and the need for repentance preached by the Hebrew Bible prophets and other first century Jewish communities, like the Essenes and of course John the Baptist.[66]

Textual Criticism[67] and Criteria for Historical Reliability[68]

In this section, we briefly describe two tools New Testament scholars use to examine and study the Synoptic Gospels and New Testament texts in general: textual criticism and the criteria that is used to determine likely historical authenticity. Textual criticism seeks to identify the original wording of text based on surviving manuscripts. There are no **autographs** – original publication of any New Testament books. There are 5,700 existing **manuscripts.** All are copies of copies. Manuscripts are handwritten copies of a writing. None of the existing manuscripts are the same. Many are only fragments and all were made centuries after the original.

Until the printing press was invented in the 15th century, texts were copied by hand. Scribes wrote without capitalizations, punctuation or spacing, *Scriptua Continuo*. In the fourth century, scribes did begin to separate the texts into chapters. Then in the thirteenth century, Stephen Langton used the present chapter arrangement in his Latin translation of the New Testament. In the sixteenth century, Robert Stephanus added the present verse divisions for his Greek and Latin translations.

Initially, copyists were likely willing literate persons. In the fourth century, professional scribes began copying manuscripts, and eventually it became the work of trained monks. Most differences in the New Testament manuscripts occurred accidentally, but scribes did make intentional changes for various reasons. For example:

- To correct an erroneous Old Testament reference. Earlier copies of the Gospel of Mark associated the prophet Isaiah with Exodus and Malachi. A scribe removed those references and inserted the existing language "as it is written in the prophets." Mark 1:2
- To harmonize passages. The Disciples' Prayer in the Gospel of Luke was changed to agree with the Gospel of Mathew. Though the conclusion, "for thine is the kingdom and the power, and the glory forever Amen," is not in the Gospel of Luke nor earlier copies of the Gospel of Matthew.
- To remove potential doctrinal problems. The example Ehrman gives is Matthew 24:36, But of that day and hour knoweth no man, no not the angels of heaven, but my Father only. At one time the verse read, not the angels nor the son, but the father alone. Nor the son was removed in the Gospel of Matthew.
- At some point a scribe also inserted the now familiar language to Luke 22:44, "And being in an agony he prayed more earnestly, and his sweat was as it were great drops of blood falling down to the ground." The phrase and his sweat was as it were great drops of blood is not found in earlier and the best manuscripts of the Gospel of Luke.

While textual criticism focuses on the original wording of the New Testament writings, the historical authenticity of the words and events contained in the writings is another intriguing topic of New Testament scholarship. Historian have devised a set of criteria that they use to assess possible historical reliability.

- Historical sources closest to an event are more likely accurate The earliest sources in the Synoptic Gospels would be the Gospel of Mark, and the Q source.
- Information found in two or more independent sources is more likely authentic. Information in the Gospels of Mark, John, and Paul's letters that agree would be independently attested and thus more likely reliable. Each of these writings say Jesus had siblings, was crucified and preached primarily to Jews.
- Based on the Criterion of Dissimilarity an account that is contrary to the author's theological agenda is more likely authentic. The stories of Jesus' baptism by John, being born in Nazareth a little known location, and being betrayed by one of his disciples are contrary to the bias of the authors' perspective and hence are more likely true.
- Based on the criterion of Contextual Credibility accounts that are not consistent with the social and historical context of first century Judaism are less likely authentic.

Utilizing these principles, some New Testament scholars conclude that Jesus was a first century Jewish apocalyptic prophet. That is he preached and taught about the imminent arrival of the kingdom of God. In his textbooks Bart Ehrman offers several reasons to support this historical view of Jesus. First, Jesus' crucifixion is independently attested in many sources. Therefore it is most likely that he was crucified by the Romans, and it is reasonable to infer that it was his apocalyptic teachings that may have been the reason for his crucifixion. According to Ehrman, the Romans crucified political threats to the empire not moral teachers. So Jesus only would have been crucified if his teachings were considered seditious and his followers dangerous. This assertion partially concurs with the teaching of Prophet Crowdy who taught that Jesus died for the gospel.[69] In other words, he was crucified for his followers, not as a vicarious atonement for sin, but like many of his prophetic predecessors, an innocent martyr for the morality he brought, and in Jesus' case his gospel of the forthcoming kingdom of God. An event that would supplant the current world order and permanently liberate and vindicate Israel. Second, it is independently attested that Jesus predicted that the temple at Jerusalem would soon be destroyed. In Mark 11 and John 2 a few days before his crucifixion he caused a disturbance in the temple calling it a den of thieves in the Gospel of Mark and a house of merchandise in the Gospel of John. Ehrman suggest that Jesus' actions in these passages are similar to the symbolic action of the prophets of the Hebrew Bible, and indicated the imminence of the end of the present age. Third, it is independently attested in multiple sources that he chose twelve disciples, symbolic of the new Israel that would exist in the new kingdom. Fourth, he preached the coming of an actual kingdom inaugurated by the son of man. Jesus' teachings about the son of man do not clearly state he was referring to himself, and scholars continue to debate whether the statements were self-references. Based on the criterion of dissimilarity, that if a saying or deed of Jesus does not coincide with (or works against) the agenda of the author, it is more likely reliable. Jesus' sayings about the son of man are thought to be authentic and further evidence that he was an apocalyptic prophet. Fifth, it is independently attested by multiple sources that Jesus associated himself with John the Baptist. Since John and the first communities established by Jesus' followers following his death were apocalyptic Jews, Jesus must have been one as well.[70]

The view that Jesus was an apocalyptic prophet was the majority opinion of him among New Testament scholars until the 1980s. Although it continues to be the way many scholars classify him, there are those who hold just as forcefully that he was another type of first century teacher; perhaps a Cynic philosopher, or a teacher with an eschatological message but not an apocalyptic prophet.

Conclusion

The acknowledgment that the Synoptic Gospels are Second Temple first century Jewish writings in no way diminishes the truth, wisdom and inspiration they have provided for over two thousand years. Yes they are a part of the canon for what became and remains, in the year twenty twenty-five, the world's largest religious tradition, Christianity. But their Judaic origin and nature are undeniable. The practice of Judaic customs and expressions of Judaic beliefs abound in each of these ancient biographies about Jesus: Observing the Sabbath, attending synagogues, loving God, having faith in God and the prophet of God, the need for repentance, and worshiping and serving God and only God. On one hand, these writings preserved and transmit some of the teachings and activities of Jesus. On the other hand, they reflect each author's particular interpretation of him as the expected Messiah and their respective understanding of the meaning of his life and death. In this regard, it is aptly stated that they convey the religion of Jesus, what he taught and practiced, and the religion about Jesus, what and how his followers came to think of him, and explain his life and death after his demise. The Synoptic Gospels also impart universal ideals that transcend particular religious traditions: the discipline of prayer, and the efficacy of acts, words, and thoughts of faith. Hence, despite disagreements and debates about their origin and meaning, they continue to make an immeasurable contribution to the "better angels" of humankind.

Bibliography

Abrami, Leo Michael, *"The Jewish Origins of the Lord's Prayer"*, https://Academia.edu.

Achtemeier, Paul J., *Introducing The New Testament: Its Literature and Theology*, Grand Rapids: Eerdmans, 2001.

Brettler, Marc Zvi, "The Canonization of the Bible", Adele Berlin and Marc Zvi Brettler, eds., *The Jewish Study Bible,* New York: Oxford University Press, 2004.

Brown, Raymond E., An *Introduction To The New Testament*, New York: Doubleday, 1997.

Buber, Martin (1950), *Two Types of Faith,* Norman P. Goldhawk, trans., Victoria: Must Have Books, 2023.

Dudley, Dean, History *of the First Council of Nice,* Brooklyn: A & B Publishers Group.

Dungan, David L., Constantine's *Bible: Politics and the Making of the New Testament,* Minneapolis: Fortress Press, 2007.

Ehrman, Bart D, *The New Testament: A Historical Introduction to the Early Christian Writings,* New York: Oxford University Press, 2012.

Eisenbaum, Pamela, *Paul Was Not a Christian,* New York: HarperCollins Publishers, 2009.

Flusser, David, *Jewish Sources In Early Christianity,* New York: Adama Books, 1987.

Galambush, Julie, *The Reluctant Parting: How the New Testament's Jewish Writers Created a Christian Book,* New York: HarperCollins Publisher, 2005.

Henze, Matthias, *Mind The Gap,* Minneapolis: Fortress Press, 2017.

King, Karen L., *What is Gnosticism?,* Cambridge: Belknap Press, 2003.

Klawans, Jonathan, "The Law," Amy- Jill Levine and Marc Zvi Brettler, eds., *The Jewish Annotated New Testament*, New York: Oxford University Press, 2001.

Knohl, Israel, New York: Continuum Books, 2009.

Mason, Steve, Josephus *and the New Testament,* Peabody: Hendrickson Publishers, 2003.

Matera, Frank J., New *Testament Theology*, Louisville: Westminster John Knox Press, 2007.

Metzger Bruce M., and Michael D. Coogan, eds., *The Oxford Essential Guide to Ideas & Issues of the Bible,* New York: Berkley Books, 2002.

Miller, Robert J. ed., *The Apocalyptic Jesus A Debate,* Santa Rosa: Polebridge Press, 2001.

Nash, Ronald H., *The Gospels and The Greeks*, Phillipsburg: P & R Publishing, 2003.

Roberts, Sharon E. Jones, *The Truth He Brought: William S. Crowdy A Prophet of God*, Chesapeake: Majestic International Books, 2021.

Sandmel, Samuel, *A Jewish Understanding of The New Testament*, New York: Ktav Publishing House, 1974.

Schachterle, Joshua, "What is the Apocrypha? The 14 Books Left out of the Bible." Bart Ehrman, 2023, https://www.bartehrman.com.

Shanks, Hershel ed., *Christianity and Rabbinic Judaism*, Washington, DC: Biblical Archeology Society, 1992.

Stone, Michael E., ed., *Jewish Writings of the Second Temple Period,* Philadelphia: Fortress Press, 1984.

Taylor, Mark C., ed., *Critical Terms for Religious Studies*, Chicago: University of Chicago Press, 1998.

Vermes, Geza, Jesus *The Jew: A Historian's Reading of The Gospels*, Philadelphia: Fortress Press.

Walker, Beersheba Crowdy, Life *and Works of William Saunders Crowdy*, Philadelphia: Elfreth J. P. Walker, 1955.

Notes

[1] Julie Galambush, *The Reluctant Parting: How the New Testament's Jewish Writers Created a Christian Book* (New York: HarperCollins Publisher, 2005), 15.
[2] Sharon E. Jones Roberts, *The Truth He Brought: William S. Crowdy A Prophet of God* (Chesapeake: Majestic International Books, 2021), 38.
[3] Beersheba Crowdy Walker, *Life and Works of William Saunders Crowdy* (Philadelphia: Elfreth J. P. Walker, 1955), 33.
[4] David L. Dungan, *Constantine's Bible: Politics and the Making of the New Testament* (Minneapolis: Fortress Press, 2007), 1-10.
[5] Bart D. Ehrman, *The New Testament: A Historical Introduction to the Early Christian Writings* (New York: Oxford University Press, 2012), 11.
[6] Bruce M. Metzger and Michael D. Coogan, eds., *The Oxford Essential Guide to Ideas & Issues of the Bible* (New York: Berkley Books, 2002), 86.
[7] Ehrman, *The New Testament: A Historical Introduction to the Early Christian Writings*, 7.
[8] Ibid, 3.
[9] Ronald H. Nash, *The Gospels and The Greeks* (Phillipsburg: P & R Publishing, 2003), 201.
[10] Ehrman, *The New Testament: A Historical Introduction to the Early Christian Writings*, 5.
[11] Ibid, 6.
[12] Michael E. Stone, ed., *Jewish Writings of the Second Temple Period,* Philadelphia: Fortress Press, 1984), 443-444.
[13] Karen L. King, *What is Gnosticism?* (Cambridge: Belknap Press, 2003), 7; 64-65.
[14] Dean Dudley, *History of the First Council of Nice* (Brooklyn: A & B Publishers Group), 15.
[15] David L. Dungan, *Constantine's Bible: Politics and the Making of the New Testament*, 119.
[16] Bart D. Ehrman, *The New Testament: A Historical Introduction to the Early Christian Writings*, 421-433.
[17] Hershel Shanks, ed., *Christianity and Rabbinic Judaism* (Washington, DC: Biblical Archeology Society, 1992), 196.
[18] Matthias Henze, *Mind The Gap* (Minneapolis: Fortress Press, 2017), 21-25.
[19] Steve Mason, *Josephus and the New Testament* (Peabody: Hendrickson Publishers, 2003), 58.
[20] Pamela Eisenbaum, *Paul Was Not a Christian* (New York: HarperCollins Publishers, 2009), 108.
[21] Steve Mason, *Josephus and The New Testament*, 111.
[22] Bart D. Ehrman, *The New Testament: A Historical Introduction to the Early Christian Writings*, 57; Steve Mason, *Josephus and The New Testament,* 35-53.
[23] Ibid.

[24] Joshua Schachterle, "What is the Apocrypha? The 14 Books Left out of the Bible." Bart Ehrman, 2023, https://www.bartehrman.com.
[25] Matthias Henze, *Mind The* Gap, 40.
[26] Marc Zvi Brettler, "The Canonization of the Bible", Adele Berlin and Marc Zvi Brettler, eds., *The Jewish Study Bible* (New York: Oxford University Press, 2004), 2075.
[27] Michael E. Stone, ed. *Jewish Writings of the Second Temple Period*, 483-489; Matthias Henze, *Mind The Gap*, 37-39.
[28] Bart D. Ehrman, *The New Testament: A Historical Introduction to the Early Christian Writings*, 61-64.
[29] Hershel Shanks, *Christianity and Rabbinic Judaism*, 306.
[30] Geza Vermes, *Jesus The Jew: A Historian's Reading of The Gospels* (Philadelphia: Fortress Press, 1973), 92.
[31] Israel Knohl, (New York: Continuum Books, 2009), 9.
[32] Samuel Sandmel, *A Jewish Understanding of The New Testament* (New York: Ktav Publishing House, 1974), 49.
[33] Michael E. Stone, ed. *Jewish Writings of the Second Temple Period*, 223.
[34] Sanuel Sandmel, *A Jewish Understanding of The New Testament*, 24.
[35] Bart D, Ehrman, *The New Testament: A Historical Introduction to the Early Christian Writings*, 59-65.
[36] Ibid, 29-46.
[37] Karen L. King, *What is Gnosticism?*, 48.
[38] Raymond E. Brown, *An Introduction To The New Testament* (New York: Doubleday, 1997), 88-89.
[39] Ronald H. Nash, *The Gospels and The Greeks*, 57-61.
[40] Steve Mason, *Josephus and The New Testament*, 114-115;284.
[41] Samuel Sandmel, *A Jewish Understanding of The New Testament*, 99.
[42] Raymond E. Brown, *An Introduction to The New Testament*, 67-68.
[43] Paul J. Achtemeier, *Introducing The New Testament: Its Literature and Theology* (Grand Rapids: Eerdmans, 2001), 47.
[44] Mark C. Taylor, ed., *Critical Terms for Religious Studies* (Chicago: University of Chicago Press, 1998), 2; 269.
[45] Samuel Sandmel, *A Jewish Understanding of The New* Testament, 124.
[46] Robert J. Miller, ed., *The Apocalyptic Jesus A Debate* (Santa Rosa: Polebridge Press, 2001), 5.
[47] Matthias Henze, *Mind The Gap*, 59.
[48] Michael E. Stone, ed., *Jewish Writings of the Second Temple Period*, 540-541.
[49] Geza Vermes, *Jesus The Jew A Historian's Reading of The* Gospels, 160.
[50] Samuel Sandmel, *A Jewish Understanding of The New* Testament, 130.
[51] Geza Vermes, *Jesus The Jew A Historian's Reading of The Gospels*, 195-200.
[52] Michael, E. Stone, ed., *Jewish Writings of the Second Temple Period*, 73; 117; 362-365;547.

⁵³ Jonathan Klawans, "The Law," Amy- Jill Levine and Marc Zvi Brettler, eds., *The Jewish Annotated New Testament* (New York: Oxford University Press, 2001), 515-518.
⁵⁴ Bart D. Ehrman, *The New Testament: A Historical Introduction to the Early Christian Writings,* 125.
⁵⁵ Martin Buber (1950), *Two Types of Faith,* Norman P. Goldhawk, trans., (Victoria: Must Have Books, 2023), 69.
⁵⁶ Michel E. Stone, ed., *Jewish Writings of the Second Temple Period,* 320.
⁵⁷ Bart D. Ehrman, *The New Testament: A Historical Introduction to the Early Christian Writings,* 479.
⁵⁸ Huub van de Sandt and David Flusser, eds., *The Didache* (Minneapolis: Fortress Press, 2002), 1.
⁵⁹ Leo Michael Abrami, *The Jewish Origins of the Lord's Prayer,* https://Academia.edu.
⁶⁰ David Flusser, *Jewish Sources In Early Christianity* (New York: Adama Books, 1987)12.
⁶¹ Bart D. Ehrman, *The New Testament: A Historical Introduction to the Early Christian Writings,* 143.
⁶² Margret Wertheim, *Pythagoras' Trousers* (New York: W.W. Norton & Company, 1997),19.
⁶³ Bruce M. Metzger and Michael D. Coogan, eds., *The Oxford Essential Guide to Ideas & Issues of the Bible,* 447.
⁶⁴ Samuel Sandmel, *A Jewish Understanding of The New Testament,* 99.
⁶⁵ Bruce M. Metzger and Michael D. Coogan, eds., *The Oxford Essential Guide to Ideas & Issues of the Bible,* 448; Frank J. Matera, *New Testament Theology* (Louisville: Westminster John Knox Press, 2007), 74.
⁶⁶ Bart D. Ehrman, *The New Testament: A Historical Introduction to the Early Christian Writings,* 148.
⁶⁷ Ibid, 17-28.
⁶⁸ Ibid, 244-250.
⁶⁹ Beersheba Crowdy Walker, *Life and Works of William Saunders Crowdy,* 56.
⁷⁰ Bart D. Ehrman, *The New Testament: A Historical Introduction to the Early Christian Writings,* 267-272.

www.ingramcontent.com/pod-product-compliance
Lightning Source LLC
LaVergne TN
LVHW020059090426
835510LV00040B/2642